All About Sports

All About
BASKETBALL

BY MATT DOEDEN

Consultant:
Craig R. Coenen, PhD
Professor of History
Mercer County Community College
West Windsor, New Jersey

CAPSTONE PRESS
a capstone imprint

A+ Books are published by Capstone Press,
1710 Roe Crest Drive, North Mankato, Minnesota 56003
www.capstonepub.com

Library of Congress Cataloging-in-Publication Data
Cataloging information on file with the Library of Congress
ISBN 978-1-4914-1994-6 (library binding)
ISBN 978-1-4914-2171-0 (eBook PDF)

Editorial Credits
Brenda Haugen, editor; Sarah Bennett, designer; Eric Gohl,
media researcher; Katy LaVigne, production specialist

Photo Credits
AP Photo: 21 (bottom left); Corbis: Bettmann, 7, Kirn Vintage
Stock, 9 (right), Minnesota Historical Society, 9 (left); Dreamstime:
Alexandre Fagundes De Fagundes, 11, Carlosphotos, cover, Eric
Broder Van Dyke, 16–17, Glenn Nagel, 19 (front), Jackbluee, 2–3,
Wisconsinart, 14; Getty Images: AFP/Ted Mathias, 15 (top right),
Charles Hoff, 29, Hulton Archive, 6 (photo), Jamie Sabau, 28
(right); Library of Congress: 8; Newscom: Cal Sport Media/John
Mersits, 22, Cal Sport Media/Rich Barnes, 27 (top left), EPA/Larry
W. Smith, 28 (left), Icon SMI/John McDonough, 15 (left), MCT/
Jose Carlos Fajardo, 23 (top), MCT/Marlin Levison, 27 (top right),
UPI Photo Service/George Wong, 27 (bottom), UPI Photo Service/
Lee K. Marriner, 15 (bottom right); Shutterstock: Aspen Photo,
12, 16 (left), 25 (all), bikeriderlondon, 32, Debby Wong, 13,
Derek Hatfield, 13 (background), Digital Storm, 1, Doug James,
10 (bottom), 23 (bottom), 26, enterlinedesign, 20 (bottom),
Eric Broder Van Dyke, 20 (top), Jason Tench, 29 (top right), Jeff
Schultes, 10 (top), Kekyalyaynen, 6, melis, 18–19 (background),
Natursports, 21, OZaiachin, 6 (basket), studio 55, 30–31,
Torsak Thammachote, 8–9 (background), 22–23 (background),
Valentin Valkov, 4–5, Wouter Tolenaars, 12 (background), 18,
XiXinXing, 24

Design Elements: Shutterstock

Note to Parents, Teachers, and Librarians
This All About Basketball book uses full color photographs and
a nonfiction format to introduce the concept of basketball. All
About Basketball is designed to be read aloud to a pre-reader or
to be read independently by an early reader. Photographs help
listeners and early readers understand the text and concepts
discussed. The book encourages further learning by including
the following sections: Table of Contents, Glossary, Read More,
Internet Sites, and Index. Early readers may need assistance using
these features.

Printed in the United States of America in
North Mankato, Minnesota
102014   008482CGS15

TABLE OF CONTENTS

Swish! 4

Cold Winter 6

Growing Sport 8

Offense 10

Defense 12

The Positions 14

Jump Ball 16

The Ball 18

The Court 20

Other Gear 22

Amateur Basketball 24

The WNBA 26

The NBA 28

Glossary 30

Read More 31

Internet Sites 31

Index 32

SWISH!

The clock ticks down. A **guard** darts toward the hoop. Defenders swarm all around. The guard fires a pass. One second remains.

The shot goes up.

Swish! It's good!

Game over!

guard—a player whose main jobs are passing and shooting

COLD WINTER

The winter of 1891 was bitterly cold in Massachusetts. Teacher James Naismith's students were restless. So he nailed two peach baskets to the wall.

He split students into two teams. Their goal was to throw a soccer ball into the baskets. It was the world's first basketball game.

James Naismith (center row, right) and his first basketball team

James Naismith

Fact

The peach baskets had no holes in the bottom. So every time a student scored, someone had to get the ball out of the basket!

GROWING SPORT

The new sport caught on. People around the country played it.

Students at Western High School in Washington, D.C., played basketball long ago.

College teams sprang up everywhere. The first pro **league** formed in 1898.

a basketball team from Minnesota in 1911

The game has only gotten bigger. Today it is one of the most popular sports in the world.

league—a group of sports teams that play against each other

OFFENSE

The idea behind basketball is simple. Players score points by making baskets.

Most baskets count for two points.

Long-range shots are worth three points.

Players sometimes earn free throws if they are **fouled**. A team gets one point for each free throw its players make.

foul—to do an action in basketball that is against the rules; pushing and tripping are fouls

DEFENSE

Defenders try to stop the other team from scoring. They knock the ball away. They steal passes.

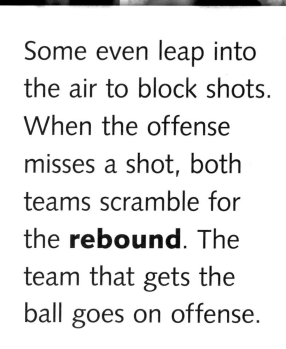

Some even leap into the air to block shots. When the offense misses a shot, both teams scramble for the **rebound**. The team that gets the ball goes on offense.

rebound—the act of gaining possession of the ball after a missed shot

13

THE POSITIONS

Each team has five players on the court. The main positions are guard, **forward**, and **center**.

forwards

center

guards

Guards handle the ball most of the time. They start far from the basket. Forwards can play closer to or farther from the basket. The center is usually the team's biggest player. Centers play very close to the basket.

forward—a player who can play close to or far from the basket

center—the player who usually plays closest to the basket

Manute Bol

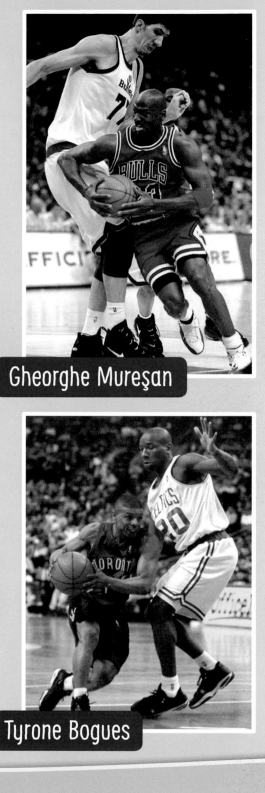

Gheorghe Mureşan

Tyrone Bogues

Fact

Centers Gheorghe Mureşan and Manute Bol were the tallest players in National Basketball Association (NBA) history. They both stood 7 feet, 7 inches (231 centimeters) tall. Guard Tyrone "Muggsy" Bogues was the shortest player. He was 5 feet, 3 inches (160 cm) tall.

JUMP BALL

The game begins with a jump ball. A player from each team stands at mid-court. The official throws the ball into the air. The players try to tap the ball to a teammate.

Pro games have four 12-minute quarters. Some **amateur** games have two 20-minute halves. Tie games go to overtime.

The longest NBA game went through six overtime periods. The longest college games have gone seven overtimes!

amateur—done by people who play for fun, not money

THE BALL

You do not need much to play basketball.
A hoop and a ball are enough.

NBA balls are made of leather. They are about 29 inches (74 cm) around.

Women's and
youth basketballs
are a bit smaller.

THE COURT

An official court is 94 feet (29 meters) long and 50 feet (15 m) wide. The rims of the hoops stand 10 feet (3 m) above the court.

Lines mark the court. They include the three-point line, the free throw line, and the halfcourt line.

three-point line

halfcourt line

free throw line

21

OTHER GEAR

A good pair of basketball shoes is a must.

They have soft rubber **soles** to grip the court.

sole—the bottom part of a shoe

Many players wear knee sleeves.

Headbands keep sweat out of players' eyes.

AMATEUR BASKETBALL

Basketball is popular around the world. People play in leagues and **pickup games**.

pickup game—a basketball game in which players come and go

High school gyms fill with cheering fans. **Go team!**

Top college players dream of reaching the Final Four.

THE WNBA

The best players become pros. The Women's National Basketball Association (WNBA) formed in 1997. It includes teams from across the United States.

Tina Charles

Maya Moore

The WNBA allows female stars such as Tina Charles and Maya Moore to shine.

THE NBA

The top pro league for men is the NBA. Stars such as LeBron James and Kevin Durant pass, shoot, and dunk their way to stardom. They all hope to win the NBA championship.

LeBron James

Kevin Durant

The Boston Celtics have won the NBA title a record 17 times. That includes eight straight titles from 1959 to 1966!

GLOSSARY

amateur—done by people who play for fun, not money

center—the player who usually plays closest to the basket

forward—a player who can play close to or far from the basket

foul—to do an action in basketball that is against the rules; pushing and tripping are fouls

guard—a player whose main jobs are passing and shooting

league—a group of sports teams that play against each other

pickup game—a basketball game in which players come and go

rebound—the act of gaining possession of the ball after a missed shot

sole—the bottom part of a shoe

READ MORE

Doeden, Matt. *Stars of Basketball.* Sports Stars. North Mankato, Minn.: Capstone Press, 2014.

LeBoutillier, Nate. *The Best of Everything Basketball Book.* All-Time Best of Sports. Mankato, Minn.: Capstone Press, 2011.

Nelson, Robin. *Basketball is Fun!* Sports Are Fun! Minneapolis: Lerner Publications, 2014.

INTERNET SITES

FactHound offers a safe, fun way to find Internet sites related to this book. All of the sites on FactHound have been researched by our staff.

Here's all you do:
Visit *www.facthound.com*
Type in this code: 9781491419946

Super-cool stuff! Check out projects, games and lots more at
www.capstonekids.com

INDEX

balls, 6, 7, 12, 14, 18–19
  jump balls, 16
blocked shots, 13
Bogues, Tyrone "Mugsy," 15
Bol, Manute, 15
Boston Celtics, 29

centers, 14
Charles, Tina, 27
clocks, 4
courts, 20

defenders, 4, 12
Durant, Kevin, 28

Final Four, 25
forwards, 14
fouls, 11
free throws, 11

gear, 22–23
guards, 4, 14, 15

hoops, 4
Houston Comets, 27

James, LeBron, 28

Kurland, Bob, 21

Moore, Maya, 27
Mureşan, Gheorghe, 15

Naismith, James, 6

officials, 16
overtimes, 17

passes, 4, 12, 28
peach baskets, 6, 7
pickup games, 24
points, 10, 11
pro leagues, 9
  National Basketball
  Association (NBA), 15,
  17, 18, 28, 29
  Women's National
  Basketball Association
  (WNBA), 26–27

rebounds, 13, 14

shots, 4, 10, 14, 28
slam dunks, 21, 28